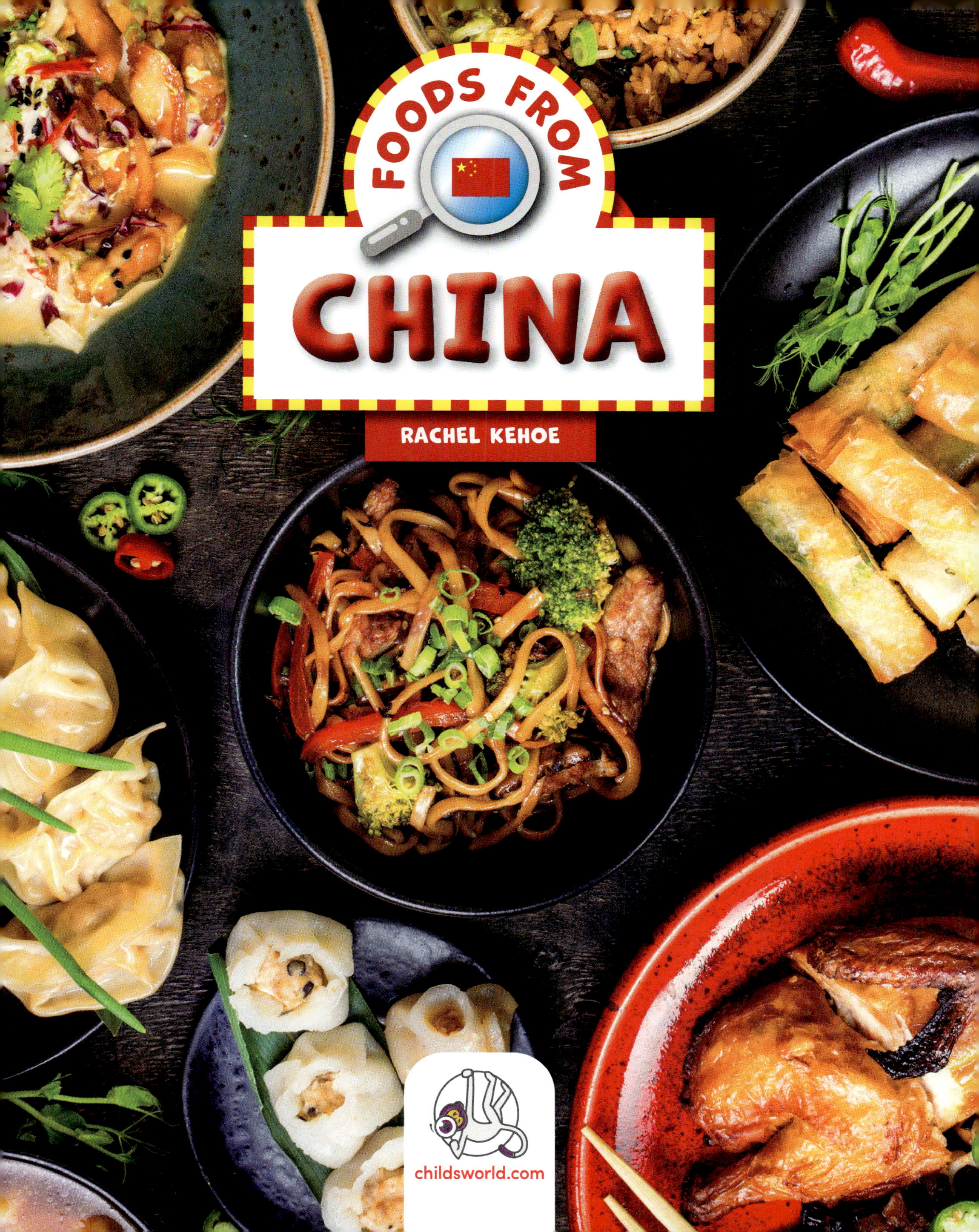
FOODS FROM
CHINA
RACHEL KEHOE
childsworld.com

Published by The Child's World®
800-599-READ • www.childsworld.com

Photography Credits
Photographs ©: iStockphoto, cover (background), 1 (background), 3 (background), 8–9; T. Lesia/Shutterstock Images, cover (flag), 1 (flag), 3 (flag), 4 (flag); Boyko Pictures/Shutterstock Images, 4 (landmarks), back cover; Peter Hermes Furian/Shutterstock Images, 5 (country); Shutterstock Images, 5 (globe), 6–7, 12–13, 18, 20, 22; Jason Fang/iStockphoto, 10; Yoke Fong Moey/iStockphoto, 14; Francisco Little/Shutterstock Images, 16–17

ISBN Information
9781503885288 (Reinforced Library Binding)
9781503885639 (Portable Document Format)
9781503886278 (Online Multi-user eBook)
9781503886919 (Electronic Publication)

LCCN 2023937563

Printed in the United States of America

Rachel Kehoe is a writer and children's author from Burlington, Ontario, Canada. Rachel has published several educational books for children on science, technology, climate change, and mental health awareness.

TABLE OF CONTENTS

CHINA

China is in East Asia. It is one of the largest countries in the world. China shares borders with 14 other countries.

China has many different landscapes. Mountains cover one-third of the land. The country also has deserts, forests, and rivers. Southern China has a **tropical** climate. Summers there are hot with lots of rain. In the north, winters are usually cold.

Chinese **cuisine** is **diverse**. It is known for its rich flavors. Balance is an important part of the cuisine. This includes balance between spicy and mild ingredients. Each region has its own unique dishes. Sichuan **Province** is known for spicy food.

Fujian Province is famous for seafood. Rice and noodles are important in the Chinese diet. In the south, rice is preferred. In the north, noodles are commonly enjoyed.

Food is a big part of Chinese culture. It brings family and friends together. Some celebrations are associated with certain foods. For example, mooncakes are a popular treat for the Mid-Autumn Festival. Whether it is for a big feast or a simple meal, food is used to show **hospitality**.

DUMPLINGS

Jiaozi (jee-OW-tzuh) are Chinese dumplings. This popular food was first made in northern China more than 1,800 years ago. Dumplings were originally made to help stretch food supplies. They are made by wrapping meat and vegetables inside a thin sheet of dough. The dough is made from flour and water.

Chopsticks are the main eating utensil in China.

Many different ingredients can be used to fill dumplings.

A variety of ingredients are used in the filling. The filling can contain ground pork, shrimp, or chicken. Vegetables can include cabbage, carrots, and mushrooms. Ginger and garlic may be used to season the mixture.

Cooks stuff the dough with their preferred filling. Then the dumpling is folded in a **crescent** shape. The dumplings are then boiled, steamed, or panfried.

Dumplings can be **savory** or slightly sweet. The filling can range from mild to spicy. Some popular dipping sauces for dumplings include soy sauce and chili oil.

DUMPLING SYMBOLISM

Dumplings are more than just food. They often have special meaning. Some stories say dumplings are shaped like ancient Chinese money. Because of this, they are symbols of wealth. They can also symbolize love and togetherness. This is because families come together to make them.

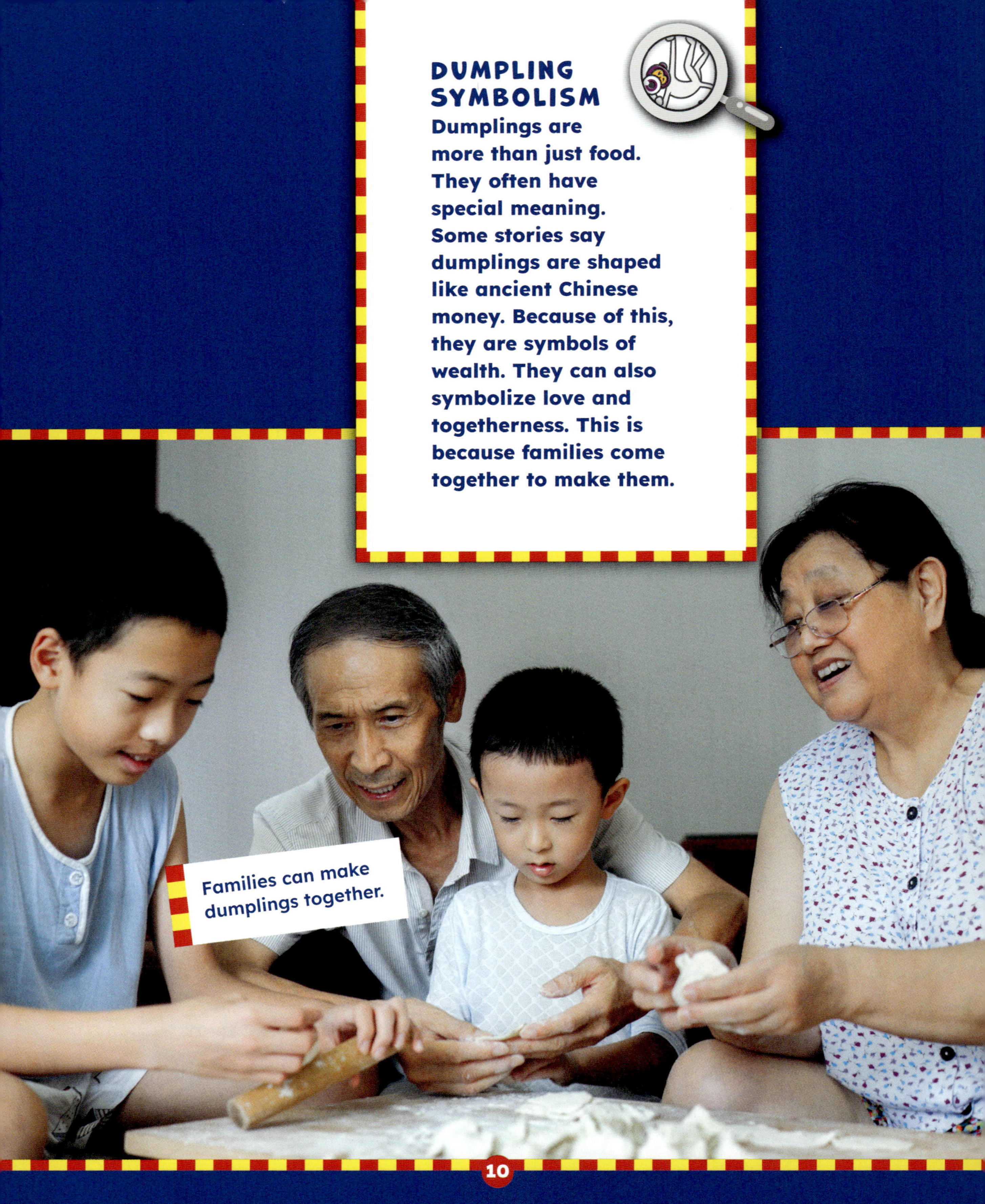

Families can make dumplings together.

Dumplings are considered an important part of Chinese cuisine. People enjoy them year-round. Dumplings are also served during special occasions such as Lunar New Year. During this time, dumplings are served as part of a family feast. Eating dumplings during Lunar New Year celebrations is thought to bring good luck.

CHAPTER 2

FRIED RICE

Fried rice was first made in southern China. The dish turned leftover rice into a new meal. Over time, it became popular throughout Asia. Each region added its own unique spin to the recipe. Today, fried rice is a dish eaten in homes worldwide. It is considered a comfort food. It is appreciated as a simple, filling meal.

Fried rice is made by mixing cooked rice with eggs, vegetables, and meat. It often includes peas, carrots, and onions. Different types of meat include chicken, pork, or beef. These ingredients are stir-fried with oil in a **wok**.

Fried rice can be made with many different ingredients.

Fried rice is often prepared in a wok.

Leftover rice works best for making fried rice. If using fresh rice, people first wash the rice in water. Then they cook the rice in a pot with boiling water until it is tender. The rice is drained and cooled. Next, oil is heated in a wok. Some eggs are scrambled. Then vegetables, meat, and the rice are added. Once everything is mixed together, the dish is ready.

Fried rice can be mild or spicy depending on the ingredients. It is usually seasoned with soy sauce. This gives it a savory, **umami** flavor. The dish can also include ginger, garlic, or chili for added taste.

PEKING DUCK

Peking duck is a traditional dish from Beijing, China's capital. *Peking* is an older English-language name for this city. Peking duck is famous for its crispy skin and tender meat. First, air is pumped into the duck between the skin and meat. This helps stretch the skin once the duck is cooked. The whole duck is covered in honey, vinegar, soy sauce, and spices. It is roasted until the skin turns golden brown. Then the duck is sliced.

Peking ducks are hung on hooks to roast in a special oven.

FIT FOR ROYALTY

Peking duck was first made during the Ming **Dynasty**. The dish was served to royalty and high-ranking officials. Today, Peking duck is widely enjoyed in China. It is celebrated as one of the nation's best dishes.

People eat Peking duck in a pancake with sauce and vegetables.

Next, little pancakes are made using flour, water, and sesame oil. The dough is rolled out into circles and cooked on a device called a hot plate.

To enjoy Peking duck, people spread hoisin sauce on a pancake. Hoisin is a sweet and savory sauce made from garlic, sugar, soybeans, vinegar, and spices. Then people add a few slices of duck meat, cucumber, and onions. They roll the pancake into a bite-size package. People sometimes eat the duck's skin separately. The meat is savory, and the sauce is sweet. Vegetables add crunch. This creates a delicious and well-balanced dish.

A special knife is used to cut Peking duck.

Peking duck is considered a food for special occasions. It is served during festivals and other celebrations. The dish is carefully prepared and presented. The roasting process is a precise art passed down from generations. It is a must-try for anyone visiting Beijing.

WONDER MORE

Wondering about New Information

How much did you know about China's cuisine before reading this book? What new information did you learn? Write down two new facts that this book taught you. Was the information surprising? Why or why not?

Wondering How It Matters

Why do you think it is important to learn about foods from different countries? How can learning about and trying new foods affect your life? Are there any foods from China you would like to try?

Wondering Why

Different ingredients are popular in different parts of China. Why do you think this is?

Ways to Keep Wondering

Many special dishes are used to celebrate Lunar New Year and the Mid-Autumn Festival. After reading this book, what questions do you have about food for Chinese holidays? What can you do to learn more about this topic?

SERVES 4

FRIED RICE RECIPE

There are countless ways to make fried rice. After mastering this recipe with an adult's help, try adding meats, tofu, or other vegetables.

Ingredients

2 tablespoons sesame oil
2 eggs, beaten
2 cloves of garlic, minced
½ yellow onion, chopped
1 carrot, grated
2 cups cooked white rice; day-old jasmine rice works best
3 to 4 tablespoons soy sauce
A pinch of salt and pepper
1 tablespoon chopped green onion tops

Steps

1. Heat oil in a skillet or wok over high heat.
2. Scramble the eggs in the wok, breaking them up into small pieces. Remove when cooked and set aside.
3. Add the garlic and yellow onion to the wok. Cook until onion is tender.
4. Add carrots. Cook for 2 to 3 minutes.
5. Add the rice and soy sauce. Then mix the egg back in. Cook until all ingredients are well mixed and hot. Add a pinch of salt and pepper if desired. Sprinkle with green onions.

GLOSSARY

crescent (KREH-sent) A crescent is a curved shape that narrows to two points. Dumplings are made in a crescent shape.

cuisine (kwih-ZEEN) A cuisine is a style of cooking. Balance between flavors is important in Chinese cuisine.

diverse (dy-VERSE) Something that is diverse has many differences. China is a large country with diverse cuisine.

dynasty (DY-nuh-stee) A dynasty is a long line of rulers from the same family. Peking duck first became popular during the Ming Dynasty.

hospitality (ha-spih-TA-lih-tee) Hospitality is the friendly treatment of visitors or guests. Hosts in China often show hospitality through cooking.

province (PRAH-vihnss) A province is a political area in a country, similar to a state. Fujian Province is known for its seafood.

savory (SAY-vuh-ree) When a food is savory, it tastes salty or spicy. Dumplings can be made with savory or sweet flavors.

tropical (TRAW-pih-kull) A tropical climate is one where temperatures usually do not dip below freezing. Southern China's climate is tropical.

umami (oo-MAH-mee) When a food has umami flavor, it tastes savory or meaty. Many Chinese dishes are known for their umami flavors.

wok (WAHK) A wok is a large, bowl-shaped pan used for cooking. Fried rice is often made in a wok.

FIND OUT MORE

In the Library

Leed, Percy. *Lunar New Year: A First Look.* Minneapolis, MN: Lerner, 2023.

Perkins, Chloe. *China.* New York, NY: Simon Spotlight, 2016.

VeLure Roholt, Christine. *Foods of China.* Minneapolis, MN: Bellwether, 2014.

On the Web

Visit our website for links about foods from China:
childsworld.com/links

Note to Parents, Caregivers, Teachers, and Librarians: We routinely verify our Web links to make sure they are safe and active sites. So encourage your readers to check them out!

INDEX